A POETRY COLLECTION

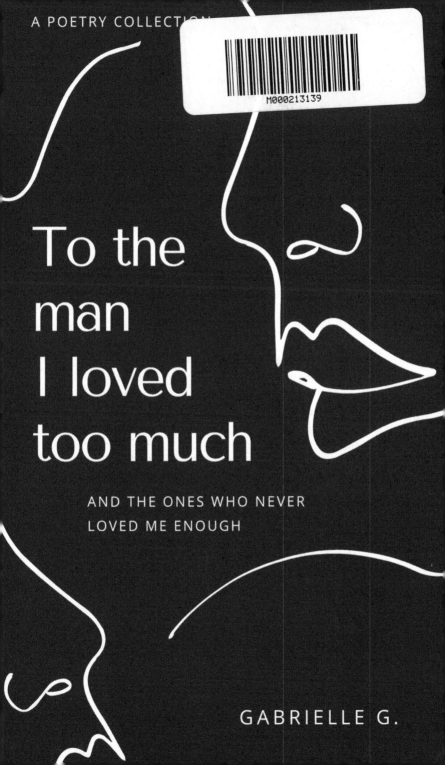

To the man I loved too much

AND THE ONES WHO NEVER LOVED ME ENOUGH

GABRIELLE G.

Cover and Illustration made on Canva.com, by Gabrielle G.
Formatting and Poems by Gabrielle G.

First Printing, 2020
ISBN 978-1-7774882-0-8

Gabrielle G.
PO 40527
Kirkland, QC
H9H 5G8 CANADA
www.authorgabrielleg.com

" To love or have loved, that is enough. Ask nothing further. There is no other pearl to be found in the dark folds of life."

Victor Hugo, Les Misérables

DANGEROUS LOVE: TO THE MAN WHO POISONED MY SOUL

"The hottest love has the coldest end." Socrates

Encounter

Simple words on a screen
Heart beating, tangled spleen
Ignoring the pull to answer
Seed planted, sweet candor.

Temptations in my veins
Resolutions burnt in flames
Dangerous game of seduction
Arctic wind, potential destruction.

Simple words on a screen,
Risk taken, fallen queen
Succumbing to the push, I fall
Love blooming, guilt sprawl

Solitaire

Hands crawling up my thigh
Tongue contouring every fold of my skin
And while you turn a blind eye
I vanish, swallowed by pleasure and sin.

Fingers entering me
Forgetting the guilt, I usually bear
Even blindfolded I can see
Your lust evaporating into thin air.

Thoughts and touch appraising
Wetness spreading down my limbs
Scorching orgasm rising
Moaning his name, solitaire hymns.

Falling

Your smile is an arrow
Aiming at my heart
and killing me slow

Love

Missing you wasn't an option
It was more of a lifestyle.
A sort of obligation
A last kiss before I die

Loving you wasn't a choice
It was a certitude
A singing and soothing voice
A remedy for solitude

Craving you wasn't ideal
It was an obsession
A dark spinning wheel
A secret confession

So killing you was my last hope
To conquer my freedom
A promise to elope
A torn feast for my demon

Suffocating somber mood
Painful soul guiltily chewed
I crave you.

Darkness looming like a storm
Malaise growling in a swarm
I need you.

Desire and gentle grins
Anchoring despite the sins
I love you.

Steamy heart feeling tossed
Trust broken and line crossed
I've lost you.

Enamoured

Blisters in my heart
Lies in my veins
Darkened fingertips
I am poisoned by love

Lost

In my darkest hour,
When everything seems lost
My only hope
Is your smile.

Fading from my shattered soul,
Tear in my scarred heart
Sinking in despair,
My veins burst.

Now that you're not mine,
Strength is leaving me
Darkness won,
I finally die

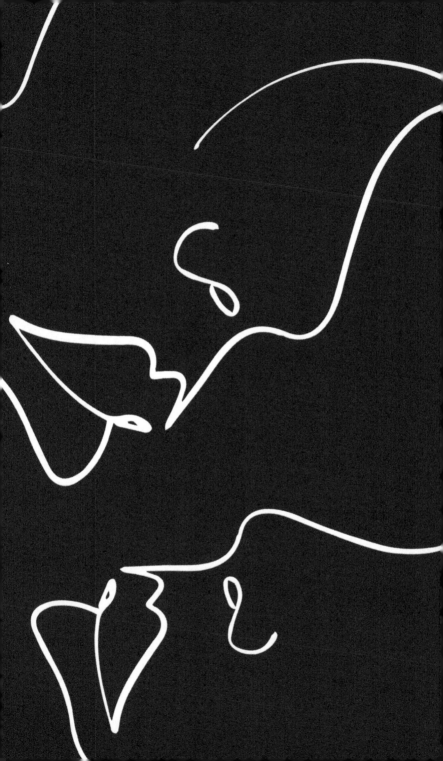

TOXIC LOVE: TO THE MAN WHO WASN'T MEANT TO BE

"Hearts will never be practical until they are made unbreakable."- The Tinman in The Wizard of Oz

There was a whisper in my heart
Screaming your name the most it could.
I ignored it for a while
Until it became too loud.

It morphed into a prayer
And a smile when I thought of you
Until it was an evidence,
I was craving you.

But it stayed a murmur
A secret we belonged to
Something we said in the night
Three words only we knew.

And then it roared in my soul,
Telling me, to trust you
A chant I couldn't resist
And just like that, I loved you.

Independent Love

Love him like a 4th of July
Freely, independently
Because he's the one and only
Setting fireworks in your eyes.

Rose

Path of thorns
Cage of gold
Heartbroken truths
Craving to be free

Dreadful tears
Guilty love
Shameful solace
Drowning undersea

Desperate touch
Flaming ache
Drenched desire
Breaking last debris

Tempted soul
Complete heart
Quenching kisses
Always yours to be.

Jealousy

You were an ocean I wanted to drown into
Sadly, it was another making you grin.
So, I stayed on the shore and heartbreakingly saw
You, taking her in your arms and loving her raw.

I stepped slowly away and silently disappeared
Waiting for a love that I knew wouldn't spear
And leaning my back on the wall of reason
Deeper went the knife in the name of treason

Seethed by loneliness I whispered desperately
But your joy was too much and the pain my fury
So I painted your name with the blood of my
     wound
Casting a spell on you for your love to be doomed.

She will drown without having you carrying her
While you'll die, soul shattered in a pool of liquor,
Waiting for fate, you roam Earth shedding all
     your tears
While I smile knowingly up to both of my ears.

Seeing myself disappearing from your thoughts
was agonizing.
It was the only reason I asked you to let me go.
And you never did.

Hurt

Was it love at first sight
Or were you my first sight of love?
Blindness certainly bites
Those kissed by mourning dove.

Ending

It wasn't a heartbreak
It didn't shatter my soul
It was a tear than made me ache
Ripping my heart with tiny holes

It was the whispers in the dark,
Convincing me we didn't belong
And your actions lighting the spark
Of the doubts that grew strong

Every day was a disappointment
Silences that told our story
Scars deep and poignant
Cursing the steps of our glory

But it wasn't a heartbreak
Just the end of what we were
A moment past dancing snakes
And the lies we both spurred.

ADDICTIVE LOVE: TO THE MAN I OVERDOSED ON

"When two people part, it is the one who is not in love who makes the tender speeches." Marcel Proust

First Kiss

A kiss tells no lies
About our emotion
Gentle butterflies
Whirlwind of passion

Chemistry on my lips
Desire blazing
Judgement's eclipse
Wakes my craving

But if need and fire
Shy away from a kiss
There is no repair
Love won't exist

First impression
Heart for a prize
Palpitation
I close my eyes

Mouths brushing
Tongues entangled
Bodies flushing
Lies dismantled

The Taste of Addiction

The taste of addiction
Runs off my fingers
Lovers infliction
On my lips lingers

Flavours of moments
We spent intertwined
True endowments
Of our souls unwind

Relish of secrets
Husks the whispers
Of thrusting sequel
From the sinners

Erasing all traces
Of our connection
My heartbeat races
Licking your affection

My Everything

Wind gusts on my skin
Spirits' darkness laughs within
Life seen through your eyes

Muted Pain

Whispers in the night,
Selfless love declaration
Silence takes over

Throbbing Whore

Thrusting is the vixen
Holding the knights' swords
Revealing the friction
Of every of her words.
But be aware of her intention.

Silence

He's nowhere to be found
He's nowhere to be seen
His silence's so profound
Let you wonder if he's a dream.

If the love he proclaimed
And the words you both shared
Were ever real or tamed
Or if he was just a tear

Of your heart, of your soul,
Of all your fucking being.
Were you a naive troll?
Is your head spinning?

Let go of all you know,
Trust fate to handle your needs.
Maybe time will bestow,
The love you thought was deceived

Assassin

Rip my heart,
Feast on my love,
Spit it,
It's yours.

Leave me bleed,
Pull me to you,
Or death,
Slowly.

Break the silence
Blood on your chin,
Be us,
Eternity.

Last drop of hope,
Knife in my hands.
Crying us.
Kill me.

ENDLESS LOVE: TO THE MAN WHO GAVE ME WINGS BUT SHATTERED HIS

"None of us knew how terribly these two fine people suffered in secret. I do not think that they ever stopped loving each other, but deep down in their nature, they did not belong to one another." Hermann Hesse

Fantasy

Getting under the covers
I want your lips on me
A brush of your fingers
Your tongue lapping me

My hand slipping in
Caress my desire
Hoping for a sin,
For a taste of my liar

Dreaming of a kiss
On a bed of thorn
A sunken abyss
On the path of porn

Flicking my heart fast
To the beat of my lust
I become abashed
That I lonely combust

But your name takes over
The roots of my mind
As I clench much slower
That my soul can unwind.

Chaos

Remove the noise,
Embrace my scars,
Choose me.
Hurt me.

Insignificant words,
Feeling absurd,
Touch me.
Hold me.

Tougher time,
Under scrutiny,
Think of me.
Miss me.

Silence kills
The purest hearts,
Let me know if
You love me.

Golden is the cage
Of the man with bird's wings
Imprisoned by duty
And bound by strong rings.

Even wide-open doors
Can't set him free
From the chains of his guilt
And the love of their plea.

But broken is his heart,
And abandoned his soul,
Behind his darkened eyes
And his need of control.

The pretense of his life
Will drive him to madness
But by removing his chains
He'll drown in sadness.

So what's the solution,
To loving such a man?
Goodbyes and sacrifices
Or spell and omen?

Because if spirits talk

Helping they are not;
The birdman can't flee
But in his cage, he will rot.

Dream

Darkened hope, craving touch
World pausing, hurt so much.

Lives controlled, cage burning
Chains broken, soul searching.

Wildest mind, healing heart
Witches love, spell's chart.

Faraway, voices heard
Spirits laugh, Dream's absurd.

Loneliness

Rambling thoughts
Cold sheets
Facing darkness
While you're asleep

Punctured heart
Wet fold
Roaming fingers
I slowly weep

Shattered love
Last breath
Forbidden trust
A final worship

Apologies

I asked the moon to guide me,
In the path of our love,
As I was blind to see.
Stellar tips.

The moon stayed silent,
But the stars screamed
That out love was distant.
Lunar eclipse.

The sun came to my rescue
And burnt all my doubts
But then payment was due.
Solar explosion.

So, I gave my sky away,
Blackened by madness;
And left you in dismay.
Heartless decision.

MORTAL INTERLUDE: TO THE MAN WHO BROKE ME BUT MADE ME STRONG

"From the ashes, a fire shall be woken, A light from the shadows shall spring..." J.R.R. Tolkien, The Fellowship of the Ring

---

Stale whiskey, saddened life,
Defiled memories, past so vile.
Bleeding scars, deep the knife,
No apologies, hurt fertile.

Ripped pictures, hope so high,
Broken fall, one last time.
Dry despair to abide by,
Adieu mon père, there'll be no shrine.

Worthless

Not worthy of your time
Not worthy of your words
Not worthy of your love
Nonetheless - I am enough.

Selfish

In my darkest hours, in my darkest morrow,
I thought you could save me.
But black knights are greedy,
And you watched me drown in my sorrow.

Inked

Blackened heart
Darkened soul
So far apart
So harmful.

Inked in lies
Selfish words
Emptiness dies
Feelings blurred.

Love in vain
Heart so black
Yours to chain
Mythomaniac.

Blade to skin
Silent voices
Killed from within
Time for choices.

Lesson

———

If you taught me something, it's that I could never be
loved.

———

Stagger

Sometimes looking for the skies,
You stumble into lies.
Remember the laughter
and times together
But never forget you cried,
And felt rotten from inside.

———

My most beautiful and longest lasting romance is
the one I discovered when I started to love
myself.

———

Useless Fight

There wasn't a bird singing her beauty
As the moon took over her passion.
Last glimmer of hope in a swarm of pity
Darkened by the clouds of her depression.

Meaningless smile on saddened eyes,
No words could mend her broken soul.
Wingless were now the butterflies
Since wrinkled time had taken its toll.

When every mirror kept silent
Monsters screamed deep in her entrails
And as the night crawled with repent
She killed herself. Welcome to hell.

Desolate

Motherless soul strolling on Earth
Red tears of pain and fog of sadness
Memories waving to be forgotten
Love torn apart and heart rotten.

Mindless body given to others
Laying down, disgust hovers
Fears of mind in a silent shriek
Screaming no but unable to speak

Darkened innocence forever lost
Unworthy because forced
They'll claim it was a mistake
But truth is, she was raped

Tormented soul of a mortal dawn
Broken wings before they've flown
Tears falling into a black hole
Loving heart turned into coal.

Words sharpened on a knife
Cold are the eyes dead of life.
Sobbing for help for a while
Craving attention behind a smile

Darkened path to walk alone
Forsaken hope, milestone.
Catching a breath, please do no harm
Butterfly rest, safe on my arm.

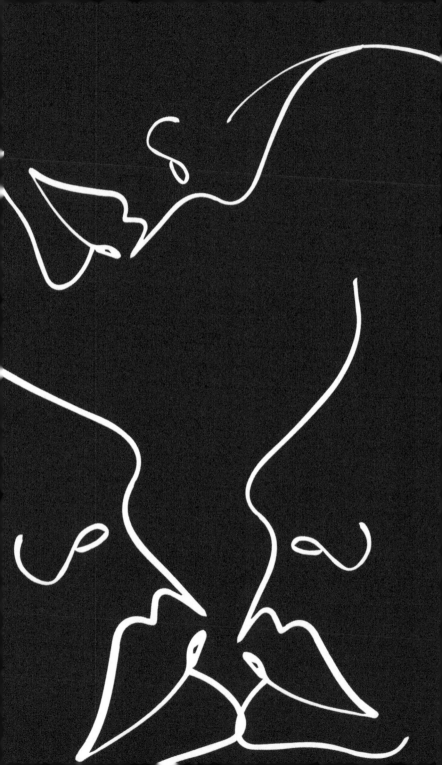

FAST LOVE: TO THE MAN WHO WASN'T MINE TO LOVE

"Whoever is careless with the truth in small matters cannot be trusted with important matters."

Albert Einstein

Smitten

Love letters
Heart Squeeze
Lust whispers
Striptease

Burning skin
Iced touch
Blatant sin
Prejudge

Injured man
First fall
Inner scam
Miscall

Soften breath
Harsh tear
Sudden death
Affair

Trust

Screech of a bird startled
Deeply the fears I hide,
To see our love encapsuled
By the ever-looming tide.

Will our lives surrender?
Can our hearts survive the rough?
Do you still make love to her?
Will I ever be enough?

Always dreaming, you silly,
Your name never leaves my mind.
Chase any doubt, our enemy.
Trust me fully, love me blind.

The Ring

The ring on my finger
Doesn't mean I don't belong
To you.

It's just a reminder
Fate strung me all along
Away from you.

It made my heart blinder
And soothe my soul all wrong
Until I met you.

The curse on my finger
Became a noiseless song
The moment I loved you.

We were liars
Trying to tell our truth
In a choir
Of accidental sleuth

We were lovers
Loving each other wrong
Under covers
Of pretend and withdrawn

We were cheaters
Hiding behind our flasks
Our world teetered
At the sight of our masks

We were sinners
Believing we were strong
Damned soul grinners
Lost from where we belong

We were fire
Destroying people's life
Burning desire
But with you I felt alive.

Your Name

Your name on my lips
Sounds like a sorrow
I can never eclipse

Your name in my ear
Doesn't make me smile
Now that you disappear

Your name on my skin
Is a regret I cherish
Reminiscence of all our sins

Your name in my heart
Is the last breath I take
Before sinking in hurt.

Your name on my soul
Is the curse I suffer
For loving someone I stole

Impossible

Every night I meet you

In my dreams

Sinfully in love and surreally yours.

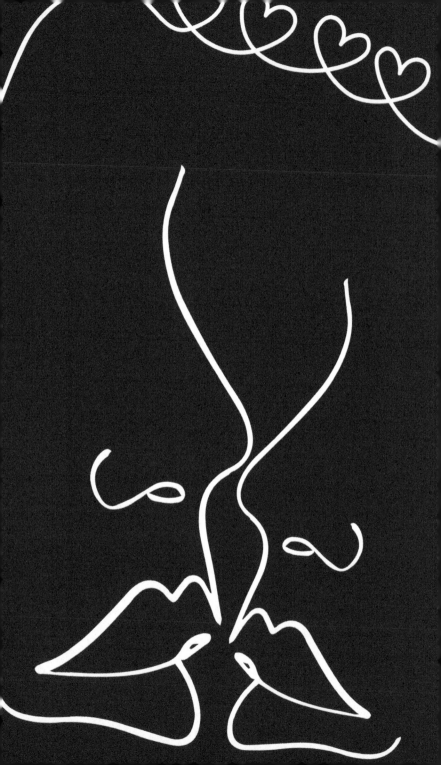

FADING LOVE: TO THE MAN WHO WAS LIKE THE SEASONS

"Some people seem to fade away but then when they are truly gone, it's like they didn't fade away at all." Bob Dylan

The Seasons

It started as a whisper
Droplets of hope in my despair
As dangerous as a spring storm
Swaddled in hail and pain but oh so warm.

It started with a caress
A brush of faith in my sadness
As glamorous as summer nights
Sheathed with desire and northern lights.

It started with a bright smile
Butterfly's peace into my wild
As heart-warming as autumn scents
Wrapped in the comfort of our pretense.

It ended up in a kiss
A string of truce in my abyss
As soulful as a winter dawn
Shawled in true love but oh so torn.

Destiny

There is something about you, I can't resist.
There is something about us that shouldn't exist.

The Language of Love

Speak to my heart
Whisper your love
Don't tear it apart
With silence's gloves

Scream to my soul
Please share the tale
Of lover's fool
And the holy grail

Shush at my doubts
Comfort my demons
Dance on their sprouts
Quiet my reason

Sign at my stance
End my lustful wars
Close the distance
Forget your whores.

Storm of Grey

Beacon of hope
Iron wave
Interlope
Misbehave

Hint of peace
Smoke lightning
All cease,
Frightening

Ray of sunshine
Sea of ashes
Lusting shrine
Whiplashes

Pink anchor
Thundery scream
Vampire
Eternal dream.

He was as pretty as a ray of sunshine.
Warm, silent, intoxicating... deadly.
He burnt my skin,
Ignited my soul
And blazed my craving.
But most of all,
He melted my heart passionately.

Exception

Except the idea of me,

Was there anything in me you really loved?

Except my fantasy,

Was I just a tale you couldn't hum?

Except being sorry,

Did you have to drain my heart of its blood?

DEVILISH LOVE: TO THE MAN WHO MADE ME A WHORE

"The devil's finest trick is to persuade you that he does not exist."

Charles Baudelaire

Satan's My Lover

Lustful eyes, broken smile
I knew I met a devil.
Broken wings, so fragile
He's become my fallen angel.

Darkest desire, cruel play
His love is rough and violent
Artlessness, passionate day
Hard on my throat, enlighten.

Thrusting feast, unviolated
Pounding ripping me in two.
Pure thoughts annihilated
Revealing my taboo.

Fate

Praying is the beast
In the sheets of love
Waiting for a feast
In somber alcove

Patient are the wings
Deployed for the fight
But weighted by rings
Crying at night.

Guilty are the souls,
Finding each other late
Cruel and harmful
For the ones who await.

Fateful are the hearts
Of connected minds
Lovers worlds apart
But always intertwined

Breast

Take it in your mouth
Lick, bite and taste,
Caress and quench your drought
Make my heart race.

Behind

Banal pose
Arise lust
Expose
Deep thrust.

Fellatio

Clenching,
Waiting for reward.
Virile and hard
Salivating

Lick

Your tongue on my skin
Lover's whisper
Your tongue on my skin
Heart whimper

Your tongue on my skin
Subtle clench
Your tongue on my skin
Sheets drenched

Your tongue on my skin
Wets my dreams
Your tongue on my skin
Muffled scream

Your tongue on my skin
Lusty rasp
Your tongue on my skin
Final gasp.

Others

Heaven of parasites
Telling another story
Desire ignites
Women coming from the sea.

Worth more than likes
But not more than their fanning
Caged with spikes
Beheaded for being loving

And then ran out time
Others took you away from me
Define and divine
Sharing was never my specialty

So I killed our story
Before hate and lies
Brought an end to our eternity
But I was never good at goodbyes.

Shattered

You came out of my life the same way you came in
Tiptoeing on my heart and caressing my soul
But your absence didn't absolve any of my sins
And I locked myself up into a guilty hole;

Itching at my conscience like a mosquito bite
I shed tears of remorse having fallen for you
Ruining what we had for one more silly fight
Seeing your heart shatter thinking I didn't
        trust you.

I fell asleep cradled by my melancholy
And wished I would wake to a love declaration
Because I was a fool hoping for our story
To be what I needed for my salvation

But we lied and never were meant to be together
The promise we once said disappeared in
        the wind
Our love vanished like the sound of a whisper
Leaving my soul to die, and my demons to win.

———

You thought it was your body I was craving
but all I ever wanted was your attention

You thought it was your words I was aching for
But all I needed was your voice as a whisper

You thought I was someone you could adore
But all you loved was yourself

———

BEGGARS LOVE: TO THE MAN I IMPLORED TO LOVE ME

"We waste time looking for the perfect lover instead of creating the perfect love." Tom Robbins

Mercy

Have mercy on my heart
As it has lost its home
It's been ripped apart
By someone who loves to roam.

It's finding direction
Despite its broken compass
It has lost its reason
And kicked up a rumpus

But the words that were said
Have misguided its trail
And as I lay in bed
Far away it sets sail

Wild light shines through
And life will go on
But my heart forever withdrew
Now that all love is foregone.

Amaretto

Dancing tongue
Spicy sweet
Heart strung
Overheat

Sweat tangled
Lust chants
White candle
Confidants

Pillow talk
Heart morbid
Broken chalk
Distorted

Ice melted
Fire dead
Tears rested
Newlywed

I see your flaws
And I love them
I see your strengths
And I love them
I see your looks
And I love them
I see your demons
And I love them
I see your thoughts
And I love them
In a few words:
I see you
And
I love you;

Game of Love

In the game of love
The only way to lose
Is by trumping yourself
For the person you love

Smoked whispers on my mind
Embers of lust in my heart
Marked promises on my skin
And bleeding words on my soul

Depict the loss I felt when
The bruised tears of my ego
Rang the death knell of our love

Sad Truth

In the end, we were an ocean of
misunderstanding, waves of lies and foam of
hope we crashed on the sand of our love.

Goodbye

It's when we became coincidences that I lost you.
So I shut down my heart and you drifted away.
There was no fight for me to win and no words to
keep you.
Only my soul to break and our love to underplay.

I had spoken my mind one too many times;
Therefore snapped the thin thread holding us
together.
I thought there weren't any mountains we couldn't
climb
But it's an ocean of pain we couldn't conquer.

I drown in silence so no one would hear it
Because I couldn't bear having you returning
Distance grew bigger while demons feasted on my
spirit
But I still loved you even when we were hurting.

I always loved everything 24
But of course this was before
You walked away on such a day
And left my soul in disarray.

Heartless can be the lover
Who promised a forever
But selfish is the one
Who forgot to cherish his sun.

Now I'm just half a woman
Feeling somewhat inhuman
Crying for someone who used to love me
And missing 24 parts of me.

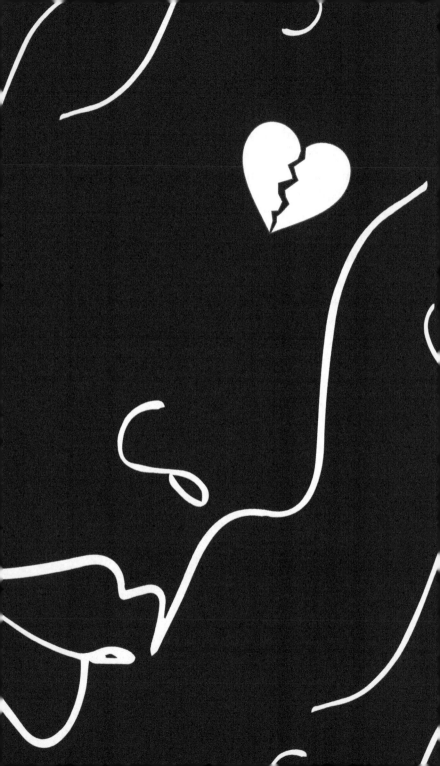

TRAGIC LOVE: TO THE MAN WHO OUTPLAYED ME

"The beginning and the decline of love are both marked by the embarrassment the lovers feel to be alone together."

Jean de La Bruyère

Fearless

Whisper in my ear,
Caress my lips
Crush all my fears
Of being eclipsed.

But your silences
Always make me feel
Fully unbalanced
And losing my ordeal.

So speak to my soul
With words to my heart
Make me your whole
Become my spark.

I love when you make me smile,
Blushes of love and butterfly.

I love when you make me feel,
Fields of flowers and girly squeal.

I love when you make me whole,
Heaven taste and peaceful soul.

I love when you make me yours,
Lustful skin and Hell's doors.

I love when you make me hurt,
Tearful marks and harmless flirt.

I love when you make me wait,
Savage kisses and blind date.

I love when you make me wild,
Savage thorns and sweet exiled.

But most of all, I love you,
With words of gold and heart tattoos.

Arrow

Your love was a black feather
Tickling my madness
And sickening my pure heart.

Angel

You thought you were my sun
But you burnt in my halo
Devoured by my doubts
And your addiction to me

Love was trapped on her finger
Promises on her heart lingered
But when his black feathers ruffled
His sweet words became muffled

Awakened to a reality
With no place for fantasy
With his third eye he looked for
A vengeance he'd sworn by before

Hardened became the feelings
Of the raven with glued wings.
And to stone turned the soul
Of the girl who was never whole.

This isn't a love story
But a modern-day tragedy
Where a girl who fell for a bird
Ended caged with snakes left unheard.

Free

I wanted to fly
Broken wings lay on the floor
You weighed me down

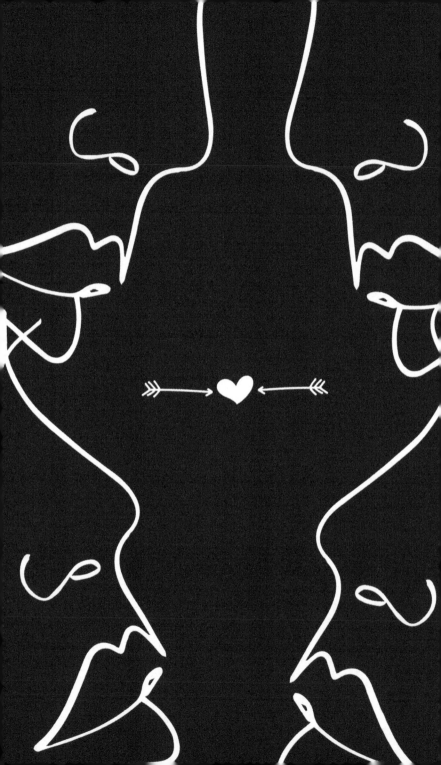

BETRAYED LOVE: TO THE MAN MY FRIENDS LOVED THE MOST

hat you do not want done to yourself, do not do to others." Confucius

Friendship

Heavy heart
Sudden silence
Treason tart
Broken alliance

Knives out
Tears bleeding
Love's devout
Misleading

Cold revenge
Cunning plot
Soul's stench
Skin fraught

Darkened veins
Stifled scream
Empty brains
Deadly scheme.

Sacrifice

The rain splatter reminds me
Of the blood I poured for mercy
I implored the Gods to save her
But the night was perfect for murder

Boring was life until I heard
The whispers and words that were slurred
I hid cunningly and observed
The girl that the devil had served

She was no one, going nowhere
Had gotten lost deep in my lair
I smiled knowing where were my traps
Could feel my pulse raging to act

So I prowled until the moment was right
Teeth sharpened, ready for a bite
And when they met her pale white throat
Blood splattered and the devil's gloat.

Murdered

The sparks became fire
But her venom enchanted your mind
And killed the hope of us.

Colors

Golden silence
Silver lust
Bronze love
You left me.

White lines
Black sheep
Grey lies,
Don't save me.

Red lure
Blue life
Purple suicide
We were never meant to be.

Jerk

My heart bleeds for your tears
Hoping we mean something to you
While once again you disappear
Muted by guilt and your sorrow

Broken I stand facing the sun
Selfishly wanting you to come back
Praying I wasn't a hit and run
While you pretend to be amnesiac

Maybe one day you'll remember my name
When the moon will whisper yours
And a smile will adorn the shame
You'd have carried for so many years.

But for now our story dies
In hurt and scars and prejudice
Tainted by the dead butterflies
Rotting from your cowardice.

Heartache

I keep hurting
But I always come back for more
Even when you love their words
Knowing it chips at my armor

SOULMATE LOVE: TO THE MAN WHO SHATTERED ME

"You come to love not by finding the perfect person, but by seeing an imperfect person perfectly." Sam Keen

I didn't plan on finding you
But that's what soulmates do.
You captured every one of my imperfections
And I prayed to survive our connection.

I didn't plan on our love story
To be written in poetry,
But you came in, all storm of words
And wrecked the life I deferred.

I didn't plan on you being my muse
Bruising my mind with joyful hues
Flirting through silent whispers
'Til our restraint slowly withered

I didn't plan on loving you,
War of the hearts in lying pew.
But Fate decided otherwise,
Cursed souls we are, but we will rise.

Diseased

If you loved me
Wouldn't you protect me more than spreading
    your darkness
and tainting us by gifting your heart to others?

Cheat

Silences always hovered
As the half words you whispered
Feelings hidden under a blanket
So I became a dirty secret.

You, Master of manipulation
With all the hushed love declaration
My heart caged and forever bled,
And my soul strung as your puppet.

Scars given by all the others
Who knew how much you loved her
My place in a cemetery...
We were never meant to be.

Prayer

Paths cross
Spirits laugh
Wicked Fate
We were not meant to be

Feelings bloom
Lovers doomed
Lust bate
But we couldn't let it be

Souls alive
Guilt strives
Egos deflate
Loneliness crept on me

Hearts break
Silent ache
Tears irate
Let me go, set me free.

Misunderstood

Screams of whispers
Invisible tears
I hurt in silence
The same way I love you

Ache of liquor
Muffled smear
I lose my balance
The same way I lost you

Dismay of heart
Blinded soul
I fall in despair
The same way you left me

End of spark
New threshold
I swear a prayer
The same way you broke me

The Genie

I wish you'd dance under the rain
I wish you'd shelter all my pain
I wish you'd mend every one of my scars
I wish you'd sooth my inner wars

I wish I'd blow on your doubt
I wish I'd kiss your cute pout
I wish I'd silence most of your demons
I wish I'd sing to your sermons

I wish we'd rhyme our worst verse
I wish we'd follow our deadly hearse
I wish we'd embrace each whisper
But mostly I wish we'd love each other better.

UNMASKED LOVE: TO THE MAN WHO DIDN'T LIKE WHAT HE SAW

"Man is least himself when he talks in his own person. Give him a mask, and he will tell you the truth." Oscar Wilde

Last Chance

I'll give you my fake smile
And broken promises
My doubts in chamomile
If you come back to me

I'll shush my feelings
Cut my own thorns
Find my own bearings
If you say you love me

I'll be the perfect wife
Proper and polite
I'll change all my life,
If you forgive me

I'll turn a blind eye
And soap my mouth
Swallow all your lies
Even if it kills me.

Footprints

You left an imprint on my heart
Like fresh steps on the snow
So I'm waiting for the pain to melt
To dance again once spring flows.
And when the time will come
And my scars will be mended
I'll smile remembering winter
And our love undefended

Ripped

Torn like a newspaper, sadly in two
My heart swells when I'm the one you send
    love to.
But my eyes wailed up in desperation
When I'm not the one you show adoration.
Will I ever be the one you turn to?
Will I ever be enough and right for you?
Do you need to be blinded by stars,
When you never show who you are?
Drowning in a sea of silence, I cry,
Not strong enough to say goodbye.
And I hold on to my last tear,
being broken beyond repair.

Mirror

In your lies I saw
All my insecurity.
You were the last straw
Leading the way to my obscurity.

The Mask

Behind my mask is a cemetery
Of all the scars inflicted to my heart
They still ooze the hurt necessary
For every love story to fall apart

Behind my smile is a dungeon
Where I keep my happiness captive
It tastes a lot like corruption
But makes me feel attractive

Behind my eyes is a longing
That you will never understand
'Cause your words are sharpening
my hopes to die at your hands

Behind my mask is another me
That I thought you could love
Behind my tears is someone no one sees
Someone, I'm not proud of.

Threat

Counting days of solitude
I heal slowly from the scars
You carved with your attitude
With kisses from another.

His lips aren't the touch I crave
But they're the only placebo
To smooth the hours, I slave
Inflating your gigantic ego

But I still long for your attention
And for you to come home
Despite being no truth and all pretension,
You've made my heart, your throne.

You sit on there like an old king
Smirking to whom tries to smooth my darkness,
But you should know that worshiping
Always ends up with carcasses.

The Answer is Me

Who is the idiot,
Drowning in tears,
When the fools dance
On the grave of love?

The End

Tears of guilt
Heart shattered
Hurt was spilt
Nothing mattered

Unknown scars
Lost hope
What was ours
In despair sloped

Drowning words
End was near
Chant of birds
Deathly cheer.

ASTRONOMIC LOVE: TO THE MAN I LOVE TOO MUCH

"Perhaps they are not stars, but, rather openings in heaven where the love of our lost ones pours through and shines down upon us to let us know that they are happy."

Inuit Proverb.

Phoenix

Rainbow of tears
Clouds of dreams
Searching for years
Found on lust gleams

Wind of fear
Screams of love
When you appeared
I rose above

Seen too much
Bled by stars
Your soothing touch
Healed all my scars

Promises whispered
Softened my thorns
Kisses lingered
I am reborn.

Self-Destruction

Silent echoes
Of God Eros
Feast on lovers
With blood shutters.
Doubt eats at them,
Creates mayhem,
Of heart and mind
And thoughts maligned.
Creatures rise,
Tears brutalized,
Darkening the soul
Of their own troll.
The hurt and lies
With blinded eyes,
Shadows deepen,
All veered heathens.
Love's disorder
Passion murder,
Corpses in the meadow,
Forever hollow.

Sad Song

A touch, a glance and this crazy feeling
That love is in our veins, strong and reeling,
A rush, a dance of our hearts and our lives
Before we both wake up from our tales and lies.

A dream, a mess and this intense craving
Of your lips devouring every inch of my skin.
A scream, a bless and this song stuck in our head,
Too late for an escape, death fucked us in its bed.

Impatient

Sadness always takes over
When you take time to answer
And I know it's utterly unfair
But my heart can't take another dare.

Stellar Hypnosis

My head under the stars searching inspiration,
I found in the dark, a bright constellation.
A whisper of stars between a Phoenix and a Clock,
A hope of light with a soundless knock.

Opening my heart, and feeling ascension,
I tried to see the shape of this revelation.
As I focused, I saw a love delusion
And found myself under the spell of the horizon.

In one blink I travelled to the coldest skies,
And fell for the twinkle shining in its eyes
Since that day I call its name when darkness takes
    over,
And pray to share the heavens of my celestial
    lover.

Infectious

I love you like ten million fireflies
So kiss my heart and dive into my eyes,
And let's explore a thousand blackened skies
Before brightness catches our lies.

One Last Fight

Stuck in every direction
Like an octopus in a tank
I feel my determination
Fading from my flank

Drowning in sorrow
Like a lynx in the sun
I shoot a rotten arrow
Into the heart of a nun

Hurt by every word
Like a bear in trap
My screams are unheard
And I vanish from the map

Embracing the darkness
Like an owl in the night
I enjoy the stillness
Before my last fight

Amnesia

Your lips linger on my mind
And your whispers in my heart.
Long after your words are gone,
I still remember, the shape of us.

Your smile rendered me blind
And your eyes made me fall apart
But it's your soul full of thorns
That became, the depth of us.

As our lies intertwined
And our sins seem to thwart
The forever we had sworn,
We dived into, the torn of us.

Now your lips are a suicide
And your love a last resort
But I pray for your return,
Shunning, your omission of us.

The Clock

Love is ticking
And when your heart explodes
Learn that hurting
Trumps all the roads.

Healing is the path
We all crave to take
But time is the wrath
Of all love ache.

Look at the clock
Watch as the season dies
Keep your heart locked
and strongly, arise.

The End...

Or the Beginning

Of another story;

MERCI, ETC.

Thank you for shaping my path and giving me the words to write this book.

I was made of love and will always cherish the ones who loved me, too much or not enough. Thank you.

Gabrielle;

—

ABOUT THE AUTHOR

Gabrielle G will do anything for a hot cup of tea, still celebrates her half birthdays and feels everyone has an inner temptuous voice.

Born in France and having lived in Switzerland, Gabrielle currently resides in Montreal with her husband, three devilish children and an extremely moody cat.

After spending years contemplating a career in writing, she finally jumped off the deep end and took the plunge into the literary world. Writing consumed her and she independently published her work.

Gabrielle's style is fiercely raw and driven by pure emotion. Her stories leave you out of breath, yearning for more, while at the same time wiping away tears.

Visit www.authorgabrielleg.com for more details

BY THE SAME AUTHOR

Contemporary Love Stories by Gabrielle G.

Always & Only (Hollywood romance)

Never & Forever (Enemies to lovers)

Often & Suddenly (M/M)

Heartbroken - A second chance love story

Forsaken - A brother's best friend story like no other.

Untamed - A single mom, a town Casanova and a little girl
dreaming of a daddy.

Darling - A rockstar romance with swoons, laughter and
heartbreaking truths.

Trouble - A friends-to-lovers romance to the beat of the
Darling Devils

Sweet - The heartbreaking love story of two invisible devils.

Follow Gabrielle on Amazon to keep up to date with her latest
release.

Made in the USA
Las Vegas, NV
28 June 2021